Down Memory Lane

John Connor with Polly pulling the cart and a young friend in Bath in the late sixties. John's daughter, Patricia Pittman, says: "Dad use to go to Radstock, Frome or Chippenham markets. We sold eggs, cheese, flowers, rabbits – in fact anything Dad could buy. Polly knew where she'd get a titbit, so up the curb she'd go, over the grass with eggs going all over the place. Dad used to go mad but my sister and I just laughed."

Down Memory Lane

Old photographs from *The* Bath Chronicle

The Bath Chronicle
in association with
Millstream Books

First published in 1997 by Millstream Books, 18 The Tyning, Bath BA2 6AL
in association with *The Bath Chronicle*, Newsquest (Wessex) Ltd, Bath

© *The Bath Chronicle* 1997

Set in GillSans Light and printed by The Amadeus Press, Huddersfield

ISBN 0 948975 47 4

British Library Cataloguing-in-Publication Data: a catalogue record for this book is available from The British Library

Contents

Front cover illustration: Looking towards Westgate Street from Kingsmead Square on 14th March 1918. The street lighting and the benches have changed though some of their modern counterparts show similarities of design. The prominent central building, *The Westgate* pub, has made way for the Seven Dials development but the building behind is still a pub and still advertises stout. The building in the right foreground has lost its chimneys and has been completely rebuilt, though in a similar style. Perhaps the greatest change has been to the road layout.

The Baptist Church has long been a prominent landmark in Widcombe. Ken Evans supplied this photograph from about the turn of the century, showing the building of the Sunday School on the site of the former *Canal Tavern*. This pub, whose sign appears to be still standing, stood at the end of Waterloo Buildings beside the old Pulteney Road Bridge and Lock 9 of the Kennet & Avon Canal. All have sadly been demolished.

Introduction

We know of no other newspaper which runs old photographs as a daily feature, but Down Memory Lane has been a favourite of *The Bath Chronicle* readers for several years under the direction of arts writer Christopher Hansford. During that time readers have enjoyed an ever-growing archive of photographs from past times in the city and its surroundings.

The time has now come for a collection of these photographs to be presented in a more permanent form. Some of them are well-known, but the great majority have highly personal associations for those readers who have contributed them to the Down Memory Lane column and have previously lain in private collections, attic cupboards or been framed on the walls of living rooms. It is this aspect that makes this collection unique and this approach has also enabled the captions in many cases to be personalised, with relatives and friends, some of whom have long since gone, being named and their significance emphasised. Their very different contributions to the life of the city are now recorded here whereas more formal histories may not have had room for them, even assuming that authors would have been aware of them. We are greatly indebted to our reader-contributors for sharing their unique treasures and store of knowledge with a wider public, and especially to former *Chronicle* assistant editor Gerald Walker for his pertinent captions.

Pictures are magical, capturing and preserving a moment of time before memories inevitably fade, when even the once commonplace becomes forgotten. A series of photographs also presents a telling social history of high achievements contrasting with a poignant reminder of poverty etched on faces and represented by clothes and possessions. It represents the very fabric of society.

This collection offers a wide range of activities from the bright to the sad, from the special occasion to the events, or even the non-events, of everyday life. It is a photographic record of life in the city in the round. That we are able to present it now is due to our readers, for whom each photograph often brings its own very private memories, and also to the original photographers, now mostly unknown and forgotten, who took the trouble to carry their often heavy plate-cameras to the scenes to record events which over the years have become the very stuff of nostalgia.

David Gledhill,
Editor, *The Bath Chronicle*

Landmarks

Few things last forever and this section embraces some sights, once so familiar and now vanished, while others remain, often with a changed appearance. There are other scenes which induce a great sense of romantic nostalgia for a more settled past, but all was not necessarily quiet, especially when the film-makers moved in. The city has always been changing.

Margaret's Buildings has known its ups and downs since John Wood the Younger built it in 1770 and in this picture from *The Bath Chronicle* files it was not as fashionable as it has since become. It was built on the property of Mrs Margaret Garrard, Lady of the Manor and patroness of the Living of Walcot. Margaret's Chapel nearby was named in her honour, but it became a skating rink before being bombed in 1942. Near derelict shops are seen for sale, though they look to be more everyday than some of the present ones, specialising in antiques and secondhand books.

This classical view of Bath was taken in 1915, according to the contributor, Mrs Betty Adkins. In the foreground is Holloway, most of which was bombed or later demolished to make way for new terraces. It also gives an excellent view of Broad Quay, then still working with barges from Bristol. The now vanished Old Bridge is on the extreme right and the fairly new Empire Hotel can be seen to the right of the Abbey. St James's Church at the top of Southgate Street was lost in the blitz of 1942.

Charles Dickens immortalised the *White Hart Inn* in Stall Street, in *The Pickwick Papers*, but that distinction was not sufficient to prevent its demolition to make way for the Grand Pump Room Hotel in 1869, one of the most imposing buildings of Victorian Bath. It was built for £27,000 after a competition between 11 architects, and two monumental lions guarded its canopied entrance. It stood next to the Royal Bath Spa treatment centre which guests could enter directly from the hotel.

One of its last distinguished guests was the former Prime Minister Stanley Baldwin, then Earl Baldwin of Bewdley, who stayed there on 30th August 1939, four days before the outbreak of the Second World War. During the war it was requisitioned by the Admiralty, and was subsequently demolished in 1958 to make way for the Arlington House complex of shops and flats. When the foundation stone of Arlington House was laid in 1960, a time capsule was lowered into the ground so that future archaeologists could recapture an idea of what the city had been like at the time. That awaits another development of the site. This photograph was contributed by Stanley Waterson.

Floods plagued the city for centuries, part of the problem being the wide piers supporting the Old Bridge at the bottom of Southgate Street. In December 1960, heavy rain raised the level of the Avon to 17 feet above normal at the bridge and the overflowing waters rushed up Southgate Street, reaching as far as James Street West. This triggered the demolition of the historic bridge and the construction of Churchill Bridge a little downstream. In this picture, taken by the Rev W. H. Parsons and contributed by Ken Evans, Churchill Bridge is seen in its early stages of construction, with a Bailey Bridge, used as a temporary crossing, behind it. To the right is an old mill building on Broad Quay, once the city's small 'dockland' area.

The city had a craze for fountains in the mid-19th century and got round to erecting one in Laura Place in 1880 (left) to commemorate the centenary three years earlier of the Royal Bath and West of England Society. It was spectacular, though never more so than when festooned with icicles. This photograph, contributed by Bath historian Paul De'Ath, shows it in its summer glory in 1915. The fountain, which had been partly demolished for safety reasons, was finally replaced by a much humbler creation to mark the bi-centenary of the Royal Bath and West in 1977.

This glimpse of Twerton High Street in 1910 (right) belongs to another age and was contributed by Paul De'Ath. The shop on the corner of Shophouse Lane, belonging to newsagent William Lawrence, was bombed on 16th January 1941.

Fires have consumed many notable buildings in the city over the centuries, incuding the beautiful classical mansion of Crowe Hall, Widcombe, in 1926. This picture of the house in ruins was contributed by Gordon Humphries, who worked for 25 years for the building firm of Axford and Smith which carried out the almost immediate work of reconstruction. The result is seen in the happier photograph on the next page, also from Gordon Humphries.

Bath has become a favourite location for filming, an example of which has been contributed by Chris Book (left). It shows a film crew in Abbey Church Yard at work in 1963 on *80,000 Suspects,* about an outbreak of smallpox. Chris Book recalls the part his policeman father, Fred, played in the film: "Dad was on duty at the time and the director asked if he would like to appear in the opening credits. He can be clearly seen standing at the entrance to the Pump Room. I can recall Dad in shot for at least 30 seconds as the actors and actresses danced around him celebrating New Year's Eve at the start of the film." *The Bath Chronicle* also featured in the film with the publication of a special edition reporting the epidemic. Film makers took over the *Chronicle* offices for a Sunday as Arthur Christiansen, the legendary editor of the *Daily Express,* produced the edition.

A horse and trap and a van cross a decorated Pulteney Bridge in this photograph, taken by Alice Bonnett and contributed by Bob Bunyar. It shows the bridge on what was believed to be the silver jubilee of the coronation of King George V and Queen Mary in 1935.

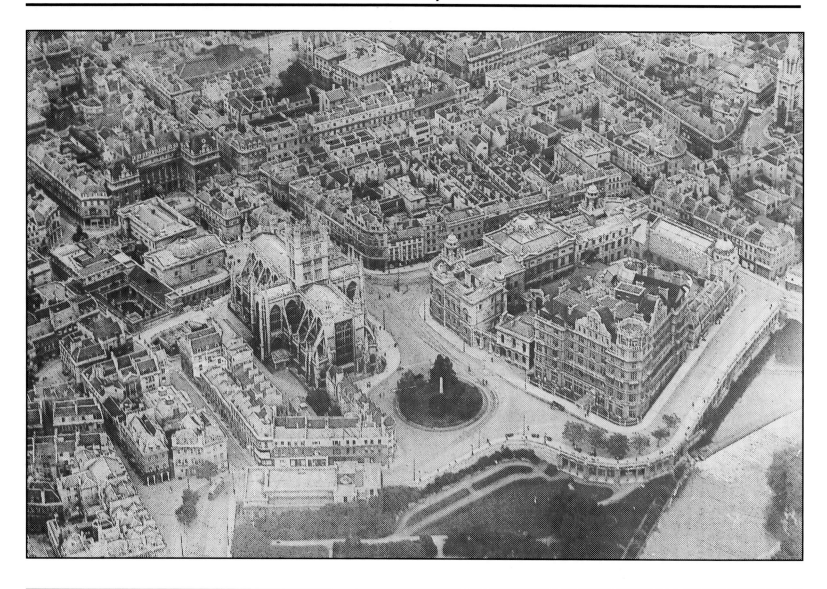

This aerial photograph (left), contributed by Lee Cundick of Tunley, provides a rare view of the old Royal Literary and Scientific Institution at Terrace Walk, in the foreground, before it was demolished in 1933 for road improvements and the enlargement of the Parade Gardens. It also shows the Grand Pump Room Hotel, top left, whose later demolition marked another major change in the appearance of central Bath. At the bottom right is the old weir, later replaced by the present horseshoe weir below Pulteney Bridge.

Many would consider this an act of vandalism captured in full flight as the revered premises of the Royal Literary and Scientific Institution were demolished in 1933 for a road improvement at Terrace Walk (right). In its defence it can be said that it enabled the creation of a greatly improved Parade Gardens and a central point for bus stops. Part of the building, which housed reading rooms and a museum of antiquities, had survived from the Lower Assembly Rooms of 1806, later partly ravaged by fire and reopened in 1825. There are many photographs of the demolition work, and this one, contributed by Raymond Tate, shows the scene from the unusual angle of Orange Grove.

Kingsmead Square, once just outside the city walls, has seen many changes, having played for many years the unlikely role of a major centre for bus or, as here, tram stops. Among the features it has lost is its drinking fountain, but that was long before its recent £300,000 renovation. It remains a favourite spot for office workers taking a lunchtime break during the summer months. The fountain was still prominent in this picture from the late twenties contributed by Mr P. Norris.

The Odeon cinema in Southgate Street was a favourite centre of recreation for years until the wholesale rebuilding of the area in the 1960s. It stood near the present entrance to the Mall and Boot's. John Billings, who worked both at the Odeon and at the Forum cinema, took this photograph from the roof of the Forum when he was a 15-year-old trainee projectionist

in the early fifties. He recalls: "A cinema ticket in those days cost 2s 6d (12¹/₂p) or 1s 9d (9p) and for that you got two main films, a newsreel and a cartoon. There were no advertisements then. The Blackett Press and the Southgate Street Wine Vaults stood either side of the Odeon."

Once upon a time Bath had two suspension bridges. The Victoria Bridge linking the Upper Bristol Road with the Lower Bristol Road survives, but the handsome Grosvenor Suspension Bridge, built in 1830 and pictured here, lasted just a year less than a century when it was replaced by a stone footbridge. This postcard picture was contributed by Mr A.T. Rawlings, who says it was sent by his uncle to his grandmother, the wife of Luke Holder. The card is dated 1909.

Bathampton Weir Tea Gardens, for long the goal of rowers heading up from Bathwick, pictured in about 1946. Kingfishers were a common sight on the banks of the river and boats were lifted over the weir by the hoist, pictured on the left in this photograph from Wendy Hart of Batheaston. She recalls: "My uncle, Frank Wood, who died in the Second World War, used to go there to canoe and he helped the owners paint the original sign for the tea gardens."

Hospitals

Bath has been blessed with some particularly fine hospitals and this section covers three of them. Historically founded on Faith and sustained by Charity, they provided Hope: hope to cure and to be cured.

The Mineral Water Hospital, sometimes called the General Hospital, the Royal Mineral Water Hospital, now officially the Royal National Hospital for Rheumatic Diseases, and affectionately known as The Min, was founded in 1738, with the famous Dr Oliver, of biscuit fame, as its chief physician and with the stone given by Ralph Allen, who at the time was building his own mansion at Prior Park. It was built in Upper Borough Walls on the site of the old theatre and above a Roman mosaic pavement which can still be seen. Originally it was for patients from throughout the country, except Bath. Lest the discharged patients should remain in the city as beggars, they had to make a deposit which defrayed their travelling expenses each way, or covered their funeral expenses in case of death. The hospital specialised in spa treatment and in the First World War treated hundreds of wounded servicemen. Half the hospital, including the chapel, was gutted in the blitz of 1942 and was not rebuilt until 1964. It also played a central role in the film 80,000 Suspects.

The War Hospital was established as an emergency facility on a site in Combe Park in 1915 and was so overflowing with cases at one time that some of the 1,300 patients were housed in a tented village.

The city's principal fame over the centuries has been as a spa and this section also covers some of the treatments available before this aspect of medical service fell into decline for a variety of reasons, though there is currently a move to revive spa facilities, even if only as a shadow of their former self.

With a remaining fragment of the city's old defensive walls behind them as a reminder of the front lines from which they may have recently been evacuated, these First World War soldiers enjoy the fresh air as they recuperate at the Mineral Water Hospital in Upper Borough Walls. Several thousand servicemen were treated there during the war, especially Australians, Canadians and Belgians. Some are seen wearing 'Hospital Blues', the uniform of the wounded. This uniform in distinctive red, white and blue became even

more familiar during the Second World War when many soldiers were treated at St Martin's Hospital on Combe Down. This photograph was contributed by Clive Quinnell, former chief executive at the Mineral Water Hospital, who says: "Points of interest are the building behind the old city wall on the left, then a truss maker's premises which was later demolished in the fifties or sixties; also the building towards the right which is 11 Trim Street, then the business of W. Taylor & Son, Bookbinders. This was also demolished and rebuilt to the full height of the building behind, making the scene we see today.

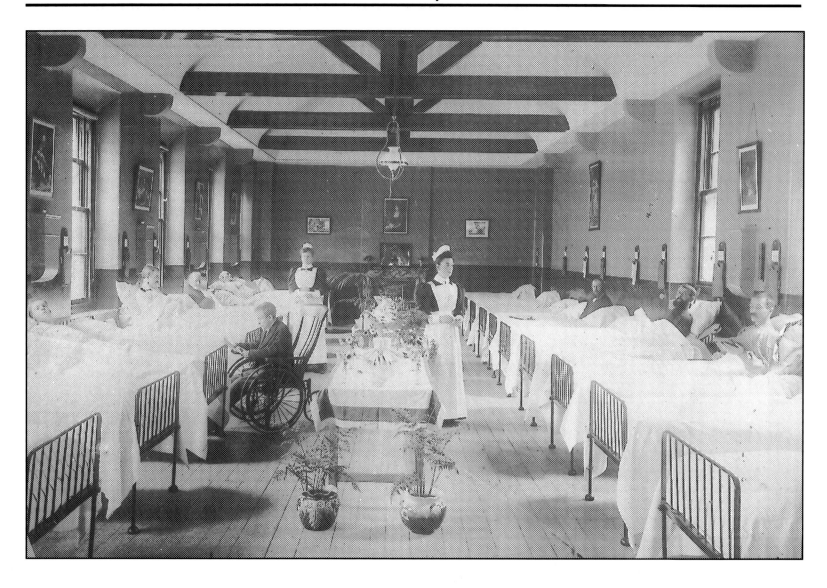

The photograph on the right shows patients and nurses at the Mineral Water Hospital, one of a series of four which was available for patients to send to their relatives. It was contributed by Police Sergeant Bob Allard who serves in Bath. The other cards showed the hospital chapel and the men's and women's wards. This card was posted on 3rd April 1915 by Alf Davidge to his parents at Market Lavington. He wrote: "I have been here three weeks today. The treatment seems to be doing me good." The souvenir card states that the hospital is "for poor persons from all parts of Great Britain and Ireland suffering from complaints for which the Thermal Waters of Bath are a remedy. 1,200 patients admitted each year. Subscriptions or Donations are urgently needed." The child at the front on the left looks very small in his adult's wheelchair.

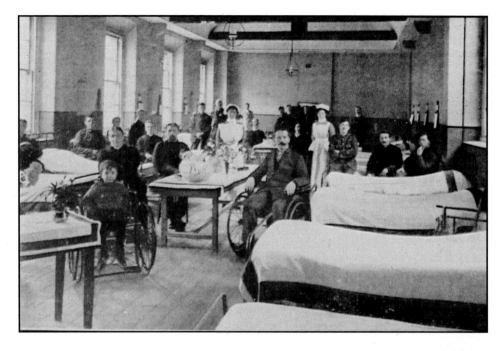

The photograph on the left, contributed by Clive Quinnell, bears all the hallmarks of hospital regime in the early years of the century, with bare floorboards, elaborate nurses' uniforms and regimented lines of beds. It was taken in the King's Ward at the Mineral Water Hospital, on the second floor of the hospital, looking down onto Union Street. It would have been noisy with horses' hooves clattering on the road, but at least patients and staff would have been spared the sometimes raucous music of buskers which has assailed the ears of staff and patients in recent years. Clive points out: "The box-like structures on the walls between the beds are Tobin's Tubes, an early system for providing ventilation without causing discomfort to the patients by a flow of cold air. The area shown is still in use today but much unrecognisable as a result of internal building changes. It is at present used as day and dining space for the head injury/neuro-rehabilitation unit."

Bath sent more than 11,000 men to the First World War and it also catered for thousands of wounded, including troops from the Dominions. Servicemen were treated in a number of centres around the city, including Prior Park, Newton Park and church halls, but pressure became so heavy that the Bath War Hospital was set up in 1915 at Combe Park on the site that was to become the Royal United Hospital in the 1930s. At its peak the War Hospital accommodated 1,300 men at a time, the emergency hutted accommodation overflowing into a tented village, as seen on the left, to house some of the less seriously injured. Many of the helpers at the hospital were volunteers and it closed in 1929. This picture is in the collection of old postcards built up by Police Sergeant Bob Allard.

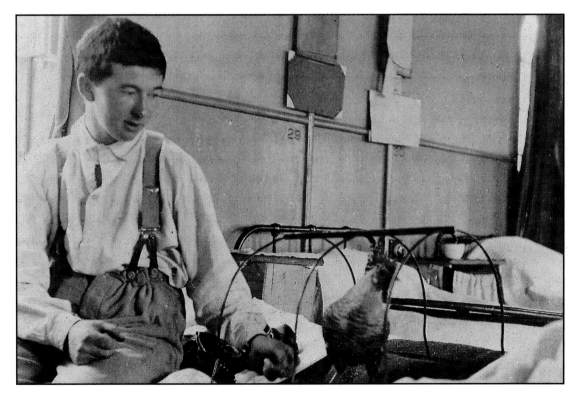

The regular provision of eggs was not the only duty required of this hen at the Bath War Hospital: it also had its part to play as a diversion for the wounded in an age when the rules of hygiene were obviously less demanding than they are today. At least the leg cage was a change from the normal chicken pen. This is another picture contributed by Police Sergeant Bob Allard.

Bath has on a number of occasions built its reputation as a spa, but changes in the health service, social fashions and a bug in the mineral water mud has reduced its spa attributes to little more than representation through the names of a hotel and the railway station in addition to glasses of water available at the Pump Room. However, there is now another scheme to revive the spa, this time with the help of £6m of Millennium money, which may see it return to something close to its former glory.

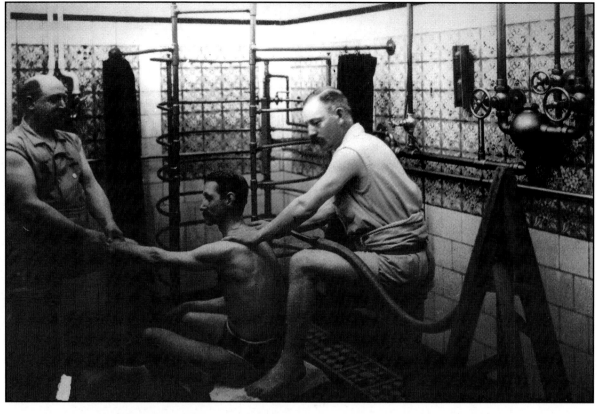

In its heyday, spa treatment was regarded as especially effective, and this picture, supplied by Clive Quinnell, shows men in the Aix massage douche baths, adopted from those at the fashionable continental spa of Aix-les-Bains. The bath rooms were 20 feet high and fully tiled. Sprays and showers of many varieties were available, with hot and cold mineral water governed by mixer valves so that the temperature could be regulated. The furniture consisted of a wooden chair and stool, with water often four inches deep on the floor. A sandglass fixed to the wall regulated the length of time the attendants supplied the stream of water and applied massage.

Wrapped up snugly, but probably sweating profusely, a woman patient undergoes treatment at the Old Royal Baths, which closed when the spa was wound up but which survived as a building and may yet be used again. Clive Quinnell, who supplied the photograph, comments that it illustrates that the old spa treament was largely passive, whereas today the accent is almost entirely on deep pool treatment in which the patient is usually active, sometimes vigorously so.

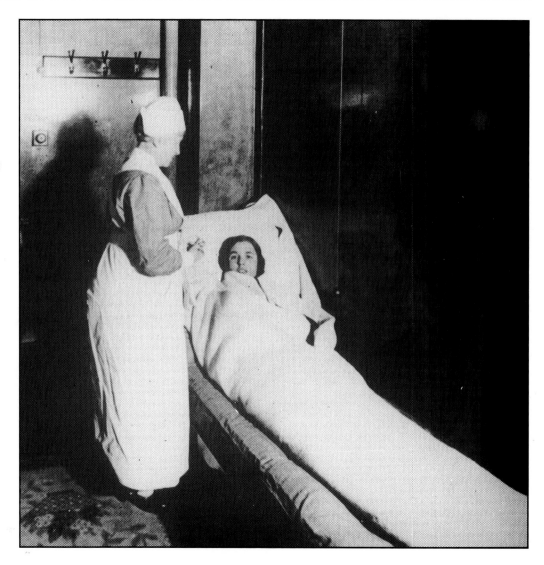

A spa treatment patient enjoys or endures the needle bath in which fine jets of water from horseshoe-shaped ribs sprayed virtually the whole body (right). Clive Quinnell says it was probably taken in the old spa treatment rooms. These were demolished to make way for the short-lived Colonnades shopping centre. There was a special entrance to the treatment centre from the Grand Pump Room Hotel, now also gone, which catered for spa patients with a taste for luxury during their breaks from treatment.

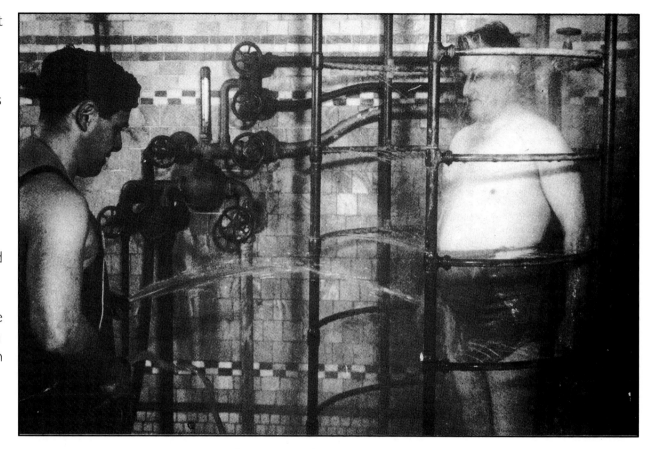

On the left is another of Clive Quinnell's evocative photographs of spa treatments which brought patients in their droves to the city in the early decades of the century. Bare-footed attendants spent their days paddling around with water up to their ankles while patients eased their aches and pains in the healing spa water.

Transport

River and canal transport in Bath facilitated some freedom of movement which roads in a vile condition did not encourage for journeys dependent on foot or horse. The coming of the railway in 1840 changed the situation and opened up new possibilities for people. Two major stations were built; one survives. There were also three minor stations; that at Oldfield Park is still in use, but Twerton and Weston lost theirs. This section covers some of the railway activities and also embraces horse buses, electric trams, double-decker buses, early lorries, taxis and a steam-roller.

Fred Brown (centre) stands in front of his giant, 1930s steam-roller. It was owned by the Bath firm Ernest Ireland, civil engineering contractors, and Fred worked for them for 51 years, starting at the age of 12. On his left is foreman Fred Collings. The photograph was taken in the company's yard at the bottom of Osborne Road in Lower Weston and it was contributed by Mrs T. Mitchell, Fred Brown's daughter.

"Burn coke and abolish smoke" urged the Bath Light and Coke Company on the side of one of its Ford delivery lorries in about 1920. The company's head office can still be seen on the side of a building on the Upper Bristol Road opposite Lark Place. The picture was contributed by Valerie Jones, who found it in a suitcase belonging to her late father, Ivor Leach, who worked for South West Gas.

The coming of the charabanc opened up the winding roads and lanes of the countryside to the general public who formerly had been obliged to walk, ride, travel by horse and carriage, bicycle or keep to the fixed routes followed by trains. This photograph, contributed by Brian Godwin, was taken on 23rd June, 1914, when members of Holy Trinity Church went on an outing to Salisbury, Stonehenge and Edington. The Bristol Tramways and Carriage Company charabanc was licensed to carry 18 passengers who had to be prepared for the wind in their faces and the possibility of severe sunburn. The man with the monocle and a Bible in his hand was the Rev T. Sissmore and the man with the cloth cap, furthest right, is Brian Godwin's 24-year-old great uncle, George Godwin, a local printer.

The invention of the motor car in 1875 changed life for ever. The first four-wheeled, petrol-driven car in England was made in 1895 and the following year saw the repeal of the Red Flag Act which had required cars to be proceeded by someone carrying the warning flag. Taxis soon followed and proved an especial boon to travellers arriving by rail with heavy luggage and a fair distance still to go to their destination. The photograph below, says Ronald Dury who contributed the picture, shows Bath's first taxi with its driver, Jim Dury, before 1920. When Jim came out of the army he worked for Bath Electric Tramways before joining Talls Taxis in Crescent Gardens and then Silver Sails. On the right, four Renault taxis are drawn up on the forecourt of the Midland Railway Station at Green Park. The picture was contributed by taxi proprietor Rupert Spurrell of Weston whose three uncles were all taxi drivers. Uncle Ted can be seen second from the left and Uncle Joe is at the back left. Standing between the taxis in front, in service uniform, is Mr. Spurrell's father, the only one of the four brothers not in the business. Note that each driver is wearing a peaked cap and that all the taxis look to be in fabulous condition.

The early double-decker bus (left) was one of the first motor vehicles to be licensed in the city, proudly displaying the number FB 04. The carefully posed photograph, with most of the travellers clustered where they could be seen on the top deck, was contributed by Terry Jennings. The long exposure time is shown by the ghost-like figure of someone on the right who moved while the picture was being taken.

The picture on the right, contributed by Lee Cundick of Tunley, illustrates as well as any how quickly an everyday scene can vanish into history. It was taken at 5pm on 28th April 1925, in Southgate Street where it joins Lower Borough Walls. The fashions suggest a television period drama, while the trams on the Weston and Twerton routes have long since been consigned to the breaker's yard. The street has now been pedestrianised.

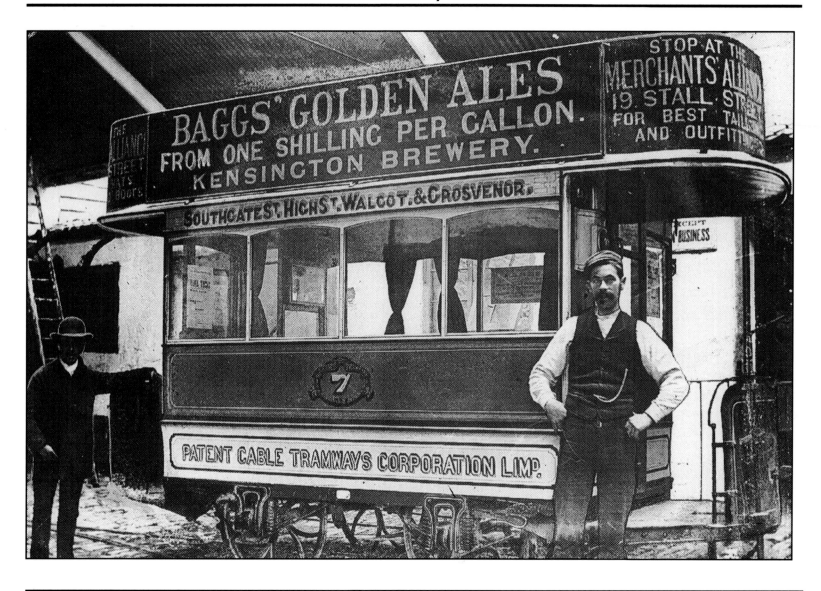

Few objects are so calculated to bring on a feeling of warm nostalgia as the old electric trams, but in fact they were noisy, cold and could get very wet on the open upper deck. The unattributed picture on the left comes from *The Bath Chronicle* archives and shows a horse-drawn tram probably at its depot by the *Porter Butt* Hotel in Grosvenor in about 1888. This was the year in which the Bath Road Car Company purchased further vehicles from the Patent Cable Tramways Corporation. The vehicle shown has had new Bath advertisements painted as well as its route, but still retains the sign of its former owners. The tramlines, which were to ambush many a reckless or unlucky cyclist over the years, were first laid in 1880 and Bath Electric Tramways began passenger services with electric trams on 2nd January 1904.

Trams and buses used to have both a driver and a conductor who squeezed along the aisle to collect fares with handsome, coloured tickets. Wilf Gingell supplied the photograph on the right which shows him in the centre, with Sid Miles (left) and Sid Bird. Taken in the early 1930s, Sid Miles is wearing the summertime white cover on his hat. Wilf Gingell says: "Note the whistle on the straps. This was blown when the conductor was on the top deck of the tram to signal to the driver that all the passengers were on board and that it was safe to drive away." A ride from the Guildhall to Lambridge cost 1½d while the fare to Batheaston was 3d and to Bathford 4d. A workman's return fare was issued before 8am at a reduced rate.

The postcard on the left, from around the start of the century and supplied by Michael Saffell, shows the Midland Railway station which was destined to become a car park for Sainsbury's supermarket with a collection of stalls and shops on the platforms and in the station offices, buffet and waiting rooms. The station was opened as Queen Square station in 1869 and served the Somerset and Dorset Railway and the Midland Railway, with links through Mangotsfield to the North. It ended its railway life, as Green Park station, in 1966. Racing pigeons in their hampers awaiting transit were once a familiar sight on the platforms, while the directors of Bath City Football Club held some of their meetings in the station buffet during the 1930s. Note the two horse-drawn vehicles on the left, the milk churn on its trolley and the splendid advertisements in the background.

R. J. Roper contributes what he calls a real gem of a photograph below. He says: "It was taken at Green Park on 7th September 1960, and shows a standard 5 4-6-0 about to set off with the Saturday evening stopper on the Somerset & Dorset. Some

rail buffs would say there was nothing new about that. But look again at the coaches! They are the original teak-finished LNER articulated stock from the 1930s which would in their heyday have been behind the non-stop crack expresses from King's Cross to Edinburgh. This pair of coaches had all the original fittings, including the swan neck lighting sets to each compartment, and stayed for several months." By this time Bath had lost its other LMS station, that at Weston, which closed in 1953. The last train was sent on its way to Green Park to the sound of a hunting horn and the engine driver was presented with a bouquet from a woman who had used the line as an evacuee during the war.

As men joined the Forces in the First World War, women slipped surprisingly easily into their jobs, leading eventually to votes for women and a total change in the social structure of the country. The evocative picture below, from the collection of Gordon Dando, illustrates the point with five women cleaners posing on a Somerset and Dorset 2P locomotive of the period, two of which were needed to haul the legendary Pines Express from Green Park station over the Mendips to Bournemouth.

The bridge outside Sainsbury's store at Green Park (right) is still used by motorists and pedestrians, but it was built to carry heavy locomotives across the Avon as they set out for Bristol and the North, the Somerset coalfields or the South Coast. In this picture, provided by Bob Bunyar, two linked engines are about to set off with a train through Oldfield Park and on to the Devonshire and Combe Down Tunnels. The fireman has been identified as Albert Parsons.

The Ford Model A delivery van from about 1933 (left) was owned by the Queen of the West Flour Company, based in Palace Mews, Monmouth Street. Mrs J. Bone says: "The company supplied many old local shops including Cater, Stoffle & Fortt's and Bush's of Bath. In the 1940s/1950s era the company was run by Mr W. Maxim. My father, Mr C. Maton is pictured in the van. He started work at 13 years of age pushing a pair of trucks. He worked for 56 years and received the mayor's medal for long service. I think that this photograph was taken some time in the thirties."

Mike Logie supplied the photograph (right) of a c.1925 Austin 7 delivery van belonging to Payne's of Broad Street. His father had made shoes before him, and he started in the workshop when he left school in 1946. He worked for Payne's for 38 years until the shop closed in 1984.

This section has dealt with various forms of transport in Bath. If transport was lacking, it was occasionally possible to walk along the River Avon, such as on this occasion in the hard winter of 1963 when the river was frozen over. Standing on the ice are George Payne, holding a bird which had died of cold, 'Flash' Garrod, Colin Read and Sid Hale, all maintenance workers for the Bristol Omnibus Company and based at the Kensington bus depot. The picture was contributed by George Mills.

Coronations

Bath has staged only one coronation, that of King Edgar the Peaceable by St Dunstan in 973. The church, which was on the site of the present Bath Abbey, has long since gone. The occasion was commemorated in style on its 1,000th anniversary.

A detailed description survives, quoted by R. E. M. Peach in his *Street Lore of Bath*, of the coronation celebrations for Charles II in 1661 when the city was also able to mark the restoration of the monarchy after the Civil War and the increasingly unpopular Commonwealth. "A curious ceremony took place at Bath, in the High Street, where stood the conduit of St Mary, in front of the old Guildhall, to which the citizens were accustomed to make their grand processions. At this ceremony Mrs Mayoress, attended by all the chief matrons of the city and preceded by more than 400 young virgins, going two and two, and each two bearing aloft in the hands gilded crowns and garlands, decked with the rarest and choicest flowers of the season, went to the conduit to drink the King's health in the claret that, figuratively, ran from it." The mayor was escorted by cavalry and foot soldiers.

At a similar ceremony for the coronation of William and Mary "bands of music played, speeches were made, beer, stronger even than the speeches, was drunk at intervals, by the loyal fair damsels as well as the loyal men."

So Bath has a tradition of making the most of a coronation, with processions passing through the streets bright with bunting and flowers. A novel touch occurred at the coronation of Queen Elizabeth II in 1953 when the ceremony in London was televised for the first time. Television sets were quite rare then, so a number of shops, including the Gas Board, hired sets so that customers could watch the coronation in the crowded comfort of their premises.

A long way from the pomp, ceremony and splendour of the coronation ceremony of King George VI and Queen Elizabeth in Westminster Abbey in May 1937, these children found their own way to celebrate the rare event of a coronation when the whole community joined in the national festivities. The costumed children included John Bale, of Frome, who contributed the photograph. He says: "We had just come back over Cleveland Bridge, Bath and were on our way to Swainswick. I can

be seen kneeling in the centre, wearing a cap. To my left is Eric Sartain and Gordon Lassman with his sister, Pearl behind him. Standing on the other side and wearing a large hat is Cyril Clark and on his right is Derek Fyffe." And so the children, in their decorated lorry complete with crowns, shared in the pageantry that marked a return to stability for the Royal Family after the abdication of Edward VIII.

A coronation leads to a burst of patriotic pride as the city transforms the appearance of its streets in tribute to the occasion. This picture, contributed by Mrs. Norah Heal, shows Argyle Street, Pulteney Bridge and Bridge Street bedecked in unusual splendour to mark the coronation of Queen Elizabeth II in June 1953. The volume of traffic on Pulteney Bridge is certainly greater than that of today.

It was appropriate that *The Three Crowns* at Combe Down should mark the occasion of the crowning of Queen Elizabeth in June 1953, by a display of flags, crowns and a picture of the new monarch. This nostalgic picture of a pub, now a private house, is in the collection of Mrs Joy Fuller. She writes: "My mother was born at *The Three Crowns* and my father's parents kept the the *Red Lion* at Odd Down at the time of their marriage. *The Three Crowns* was in the family for more than 100 years."

Celebrity Occasions

The city has long played host to Royalty and the famous, sometimes in troubled times but more often as the centre of high celebration. Visits have been formal on occasions and sometimes relaxed, as in the Queen's extended walkabout in 1977; other visits have been private, just to see friends or to see the sights.

On the right, Field Marshal Douglas Haig, who was rewarded with an earldom for his role as commander-in-chief of the British forces in the bitter war of attrition in Flanders and France during the First World War, and who achieved further and perhaps more lasting fame as founder of Poppy Day, paid a peaceful visit to the Roman Baths in the company of the Mayor and Mayoress, Alderman and Mrs Cedric Chivers, who are seen together in this Lee Cundick photograph.

The date was 22nd September 1910 when Sir George McAlpine was guest of honour at the stone-laying ceremony at Widcombe Baptist Chapel in the era when straw hats, bowlers and toppers were all the fashion. This picture of so many characters clustered together amid the scaffolding is in the collection of Stephen Lord.

(left) Blitzed cities in the Second World War often received a morale-boosting visit from the King and Queen whose own Buckingham Palace had been bombed. It was on such an occasion that Bath, long familiar with Royal visits, received its most celebrated visit shortly after the two nights of bombing in April 1942. The recently restored Assembly Rooms were gutted by fire-bombs, but from the burning building had been dragged this wheeled Sedan chair which provided an almost elegant diversion amid the surrounding debris. Lee Cundick, of Tunley, from whose collection this picture comes, comments: "The King and Queen chatted to many people who were in the raids and inspected many treasures recovered from the ruins."

A beaming Winston Churchill, with the cares of being Prime Minister behind him for a time, received the Freedom of the City in 1950. Miss Kathleen Harper, Bath's first woman mayor, looked equally happy in this picture contributed by Edmund Murray who served as Sir Winston's bodyguard from 1950 until his death in 1965.

The bells of Bath Abbey almost drowned out the words of the city's new Freeman as he spoke at a luncheon in his honour at the Guildhall in reply to the mayor's tribute. The latter had said: "Never has anyone more richly deserved the lasting place in history which is assured to you; never has anyone more justly merited the gratitude and affection of freedom-loving people of the world; never can anyone have been admitted a Freeman of the city with greater goodwill, sincerity and admiration."

Second World War and V-E Day Parties

The Second World War was to affect Bath in much the same way as every other town in the Kingdom, but it also transformed the city permanently. September 1939 saw the closure of the great spa hotels as they became the temporary quarters for hundreds of civil servants and sailors when the Admiralty moved in to what were then deemed safer surroundings than London. The Admiralty stayed on after the war, moving in time to newly-constructed offices, and even now provides employment for many Bath workers.

That the city was not so safe was proved decisively on the nights of 25th-26th April 1942 when the German Luftwaffe struck in its series of Baedeker raids. The bombers left more than 400 dead, hundreds more injured, and over 1,000 shops, churches and houses destroyed, with more than 19,000 damaged to some extent.

After nearly five years of war in Europe, victory came at last in May 1945. It was greeted with wild enthusiasm, hundreds of bonfires and the rocking of cars which were rash enough to take to the streets. More sedately there were street parties in almost every area, children being given the favoured places at the long tables even if the fare was spartan by today's standards as rationing was still tightening belts everywhere.

As the Second World War ground on its dreadful way and food supplies dwindled from mounting losses of shipping, the slogan "Dig for Victory" caught hold of the public imagination and flower beds were turned into vegetable patches. But the digging illustrated here, contributed by Kathleen Smith, had much greater urgency about it: people were digging shelters for their families and friends as the theory that the bomber would always get through took root.

In the example on the right, a shelter was being dug by women for school children. Kathleen Smith recalls: "The head teacher of St Saviour's Junior School in Larkhall, Mr Frank Garroway, said he wanted an air raid shelter built. He asked me and some other women help him remove the earth. This picture, with me on the far left and Mrs Sharp in the centre, shows the shelter after most of the earth had been removed." Shelters did save many lives, but were also to prove death traps; there were several cases of great carnage in devastated shelters in Bath.

Bombed houses, gallant, exhausted rescue workers and the stunned homeless left staring at the ruins provided an all too common sight after the German bombing blitz on Bath during the two nights of 25th and 26th April 1942. This scene, from Bath Reference Library archives, shows King Edward Road, Oldfield Park, after the German planes had left for the temporary security of their bases in France.

Victory in Europe in May 1945 gave a long-awaited excuse for a celebration, though the war against Japan was to drag on until August. This street party scene in Clarence Street, Walcot, was contributed by Patricia Coleman of Bath. Because of the steepness of the street, tea was laid out on tables in the front gardens of the houses. The photograph was taken outside No.19 with the owner, Jon Gunning standing in the doorway. Patricia Coleman recalls other people in the street as Mabel Powell, Peggy Chipper, Tony Powell, Edgar Coleman, Peter Latham, Jenny Latham, Brenda Leaky, Madie Coleman, Janet Minto, Teddy Jones, Zena Jones, Pat Coleman, Roger and Michael Flint, Rodney Towers, Alan Brewer, Sidney Gunning and Maurice Glisson.

Fancy dress reflected the light-hearted mood in this VE-day party at Bruton Avenue. Joyce Brooke recalls: "My three sisters, brother and I had a very exciting day. Most of us dressed up. We had a party and paraded in the streets. This picture was taken at the back of Bruton Avenue, just off Bear Flat where we lived. We also had friends from Beechen Cliff to join in. We were just one, big, happy family in those days."

"There was not a lot on the table because of wartime rationing", says Diana Book of Bath, describing this VE-Day street party scene at Batheaston. Diana, who was then Diana Russell, can be seen sitting at the head of the table on the right. Her sister, Patricia, is behind and her elder sister, Barbara, is fifth in from the left. It was a day to remember, a day when the flags came out.

Floods

Floods were the curse of Bath for many centuries, especially as the city began to expand outside its medieval walls to the river meadows and marshes beyond. They were sometimes spectacular, but most years they caused disruption in some measure and often serious damage. The Recreation Ground was usually the first to suffer, with the flood water inundating the Convent School beyond. The residents of Dolemeads and Twerton became used to being rescued by boats as the Avon burst its banks. After the drama was over, hundreds of cellars in the city centre would still be under water and their contents ruined yet again. Many people just abandoned their cellars for good..

The 1960s saw such serious flooding that it was decided that "something must be done". The Old Bridge, the principal crossing point over the Avon for centuries, was considered to be a major culprit with its wide piers acting as a block to the flood waters. It was removed and the Churchill Bridge built in its place, further downstream and wider, to accommodate the increased number of vehicles. The old Pulteney Weir was replaced by the present horseshoe weir and lock gates were constructed alongside it and at Twerton so that the river's flow could be better controlled. The banks of the Avon were also cleaned up to reduce obstructions and in many cases rebuilt. So far it has worked and the city's floods have receded into the realms of nostalgia, certainly better to look back upon than to endure at the time. The levels of many of the worst floods over the years can still be seen carved into the south pier of the Halfpenny Footbridge behind the railway station serving, as a reminder of the devastations of the past.

The arms of the cranes on Broad Quay look like masts of submerged wrecks as the floods deepen in the area of the Old Bridge at the bottom of Southgate. This dramatic scene, from the collection of Hylton Bayntun-Coward, was almost at the height of the floods in 1894 with the river water just poised to wash across the bridge. It took another 70 years, but the death knell was already ringing for this bridge which was held partly responsible for the frequent floods in the city.

Policemen manned a punt to rescue residents and ferry supplies as flood waters engulfed the Lower Bristol Road in 1947. Mrs G. Jones of Twerton was ten and her parents are looking out of the open window. She recalls: "The back of the house was a foot or so lower than the front which meant the kitchen was several feet under water. There was no way of cooking a meal so as soon as the water had subsided we were taken to Oldfield School for a hot meal."

As a means of transport it was at least different, the only consolation for people being ferried from their flooded homes in the Dolemeads, along Pulteney Road to dry land at Caroline Buildings. Adrian Wallace contributed this picture of his friend Keith Rippin on his mission of mercy in 1960. He says: "I could not get to work at the Golden Valley Paper Mills in Bitton as Bitton, along with Swineford, was cut off and the mill was severely flooded. Instead I helped Keith bring some of the Dolemeads residents to dry land."

People are forced upstairs for safety as flood waters rush through James Street West (below). S. Lee of Southdown prizes this unusual record of her mother. She recalls: "The level of the water can be seen at No. 32. No. 31 had four steps leading up to the front door, so it seems that it was not so badly affected, but of course the gardens and other rooms at the back were flooded as were the gardens of New King Street. My mother, Mrs Durbin, lived at No. 31 and can be seen with Mrs Kettlety, while Mr and Mrs Jackson are at No. 32."

The Rev W. H. Parsons of Widcombe Baptist Church captured many unusual views of Bath with his camera and this one (right), from the collection of Ken Evans, must rank among his most telling as the 1964 flood water, 20ft above normal, rose to the rooftops. The picture shows the top of Bath Cricket Club's old pavilion, with the Dolemeads in the background and the Royal Mail sorting office across the river

There was a sense of urgency as a squad built and maintained a dam to keep the flood waters out of the *Larkhall Inn* during one of the regular inundations in the 1960s. The picture was contributed by Grace Harper, who was licensee of the inn for many years with her husband Tom, who died in 1975.

Schools

It is arguable that there is no more telling pictorial commentary on social changes than can be shown in school group photographs, and it may be felt that some of the pictures here illustrate that point. Some of the scenes suggest how hard times could be, but most also show a sense of pride for both teachers and pupils as young, lifelong friendships were forged and futures mapped out.

It seems a long way from a 'scholar's slate' to the computer as a learning tool, but the essence of the exercise is still the same. The slate certainly pulls the viewer up with a jolt as a reminder of just how sweeping changes have been over so short a time. In this picture, nine-year-old Jack Grinter proudly records that he had not missed school during the year ended on 31st May 1913. Jack became a carpenter after he left school at 14 and examples of his craftsmanship are to be found in many of the bungalows along Warminster Road. His mother kept a guest house in The Paragon. He was still working his Oldfield Lane allotment into his nineties. This record of achievement was contributed by his son, Michael.

At first glance this looks like any other school photograph but it is actually made up of ten sets of twins photographed about 1935 in St Luke's (now St Philip's) School playground. The contributor, Gordon Rumble, of Dunkerton, remembers some of the names as, back row, left to right, Raymond and Kenneth Milsom, Peter and Gordon Rumble, Josie and Sonny Cassey, Joan and Betty Gilbert and Molly Roper. The front row includes Tony Roper, the Sellicks, the Wooleys, the Earleys, and Esme and Michael Lodge.

On the right, Miss Murphy stands proudly with her class of 1920-21 at St John's Roman Catholic Infants' School at South Parade, part of which has since been converted to flats. Ron Lancaster-Smith, who lived in Bath before moving to Hastings, is third from the left in the front row with his sister, Bernadine, behind him. He says: "On the left is Vincent Mancini with the plant pot. Others include Mervyn Schofield and Cuthbert Rosenthal. Cuthbert died in an accident at Prior Park in the 1920s."

"There were as many as 50 pupils in a class, but we all had a good education", recalls Kenneth Yeo of his days at East Twerton School. The children in Polly Clapp's class, row upon row, look alertly at the camera as she slightly raises her eyes to heaven.

The photographer did not charm too many broad smiles out of these children of South Twerton School when the time came for their class to be recorded for posterity in 1929. Mrs K. P. Offer who contributed the picture, had a place in the all girls' row and she remembers many of the names. These include, in the back row: Roy Maggs, Roger Mins, Eric Palmer and

Bill Perry; in the next row: Ken Norris, Gerald Evans, Gordon Dore, Oliver Robinson and George Hauser; in the all girls' row: Kathleem Deem, Monica Cox, Gwen Little, Phyllis Dole and Valerie Noble; and in the bottom row: Dennis Boyce, Jean Withey, Nancy Short, Hazel Tanner and John Smale.

Characters

Characters are seemingly always in short supply. The last of
them are always dying out, yet each generation comes up with
a new wave. A character has been defined unkindly as a
person with a licence to be rude, but more kindly as a person
whose talents, often humble, make him stand out from the
crowd. Sometimes they are leaders, but more often they are
people who merely have the gift to tell a good yarn or dress in
an old-fashioned way. In any event, they catch the eye and are
remembered beyond their time. Usually they revel in their
status and often rightly so.

On the right, a bowler-hatted young man stares confidently
out of the picture, contributed by John Symonds. He was
Frank Perry, who died in 1972, and is remembered as one of
the great characters of the city. He began work as a platform
boy on the railways before graduating to dining cars on the
run from Bath to the North. This experience qualified him for
his next step up the catering ladder as head waiter at both the
Grand Pump Room Hotel and the Empire Hotel, centres of
the tourist and spa life of the city until the Second World War.
His stories of those days were legion.

Two of the old salesmen characters of Bath live on in the photographic collection of Betty Adkins. The bearded man in the picture on the left is Guinea Pig Jack, photographed at the turn of the century in Manvers Street, while the other is Blind Teddy who traded his wares outside the Holburne Museum.

It seems a far cry from political activism, but this tranquil scene at Eagle House, Batheaston, represents its flowering. Bill Calderhead, secretary and archivist of the Batheaston Society, put this picture on view at the centenary celebrations of Batheaston Parish Council. It was taken by Lt Col Linley Blathwayt, who lived at Eagle House from

1882 until his death in 1919, and made his home a centre for the recuperation of campaigners in the women's suffrage movement, the building in the background being specially adapted for them. The photograph shows Adela Pankhurst (left), youngest daughter of Mrs Emmeline Pankhurst, leader of the movement which eventually helped to win votes for women, with Annie Kenney beside a tree planted at Eagle House by Mrs Pankhurst on 16th April 1910.

A celebrated polio patient at St Martin's Hospital, Bath, regularly received some 900 Christmas cards, as well as gifts, from past and present patients, visitors and staff, during the 36 years she spent at the hospital. Beatrice Beadle, known to the world as "Bee", contracted polio as a child and was treated at various hospitals all over Britain until she was finally admitted to St Martin's in 1944. She stayed there until her death, aged 68, in 1980. She was legendary for her fortitude in suffering and underwent a total of 51 operations. She became a skilled dressmaker and embroiderer, making bridesmaid's and christening outfits for staff at the hospital. When her Premium Bond 'came up', she gave away her winnings within half an hour.

Music

The city has a rich musical reputation, dominated in recent years, perhaps, by the Bath Festival, Menuhin and Tippett. And during the Second World War, the Big Bands used to perform to a packed Pavilion on Sunday evenings. But there have also been other musical traditions which never caught the headlines in quite the same way. The star attractions came and went to their next big billing, but the local musicians played on to their no less devoted supporters. Here we look at some of them.

This uniformed band was aptly and proudly named the Radstock Silver Prize Band and in this 1935 photograph displays some of the trophies it had won. Mrs Nellie Gait, whose husband, Clarence, third from the left in the middle row, played the cornet, recalls Sunday afternoons in the season at the Parade Gardens when the band used to entertain the crowds.

Eddie Dunn, who reigned supreme over the music scene in Bath during the 1930s until he retired to South Africa, sits confidently with his musicians in this photograph of the Pump Room Orchestra contributed by Pam Hawker. Her Italian grandfather, Joseph Bossi, who played trumpet with the orchestra for 50 years, is in the back row, second from the left. The orchestra, founded in the 1880s, was in existence until 1938 when it was disbanded by the city council. Its exhausting schedule included symphony concerts on Monday and Tuesday evenings and on Tuesday afternoons, with two more concerts with soloists on Wednesdays. There were concerts every morning and afternoon, while three members of the orchestra formed the Pump Room Trio to play during coffee and teatime. Monday night was happy night when every seat cost only 6d.

Jean Whitaker, now of Westbury, sits at the piano in her photograph of Ron Stewart's Spa Sweet Swing at Combe Down Village Hall in August 1942. She says: "I must have been about 15 when I answered an advertisement in *The Bath Chronicle* for people interested in forming a band. Bill Donovan held auditions at St John's Roman Catholic Church and the band played numerous gigs, the line-up changing as members were called up for the war." She vividly recalls the night of 25th April 1942, when the band was playing at Winsley Village Hall. "When the sirens went off no-one took much notice and just went on dancing. Then we heard the crumps which got ever louder and a piece of plaster fell from the ceiling and landed on top of the piano. The dance continued but we were told Bath was under attack. Our middle-aged taxi driver refused to take us to Bath and we had to find another. From the top of Combe Down it seemed as if the whole of Bath was on fire."

Robin Benton, music coordinator at the school, started Moorlands Junior School Band in 1975 and his picture was taken in its second year. Today some 40 children make up the band which plays at fetes and concerts in the Bath area. Some of the young musicians have gone on to play in senior orchestras and wind bands, while others have been sufficiently inspired by their youthful experience to study at the Royal College of Music in London. In the picture, from left to right, are Sarah Cutland (clarinet), Karen Hawkins (percussion), David Metelko and Andrew Isaac (trombones) and Kevin Hamilton (euphonium).

Entertainments and Excursions

Groups love special occasions — those celebrations under the name of a carnival, an excursion, a production or even a good old fete; anything that lifts life out of the ordinary. Sometimes they rank as the main justification for the existence of an organisation, but mostly they are an add-on, a bonus, as it were, for staying the course. What marks them out now is their essential simplicity, an unsophisticated enjoyment of life when old friends can be reunited, at least in memory.

The location on the right, beautiful as it is with a weir splashing behind, is now unknown, but it was the destination of Batheaston Church choir in the 1890s when fashion dictated that they should be dressed just as formally on an excursion as in the choir stalls. The Rev A. M. 'Dapper' Downes, the vicar of Batheaston from 1888 to 1928, is on the left of the group. The photograph was used as one of the illustrations at an exhibition to mark the centenary of Batheaston Parish Council.

Most of the great stars of music hall entertained at the former Palace Theatre, Sawclose, Bath, during the first half of this century in twice-nightly performances before the tradition died and bingo took over. Doris Stuckey, of Midsomer Norton, values this picture which shows her father, Joseph Sellman, fourth from left, with a rather severe looking group outside the theatre. The reason for the gathering is sadly not known. She recalls that her father, who

had been a platelayer for the LMS Railway and had been one of the founders of Bath City Amateurs, was well-known in local footballing circles. He later ran the Palace Theatre. On one occasion, when a group of lions took part in a show there, they were housed, when off-duty, in a cage at *The Bath Chronicle*.

The prospect of rain is the perpetual threat to every organiser planning an outdoor celebration in an English summer and it was clearly a wet day in the photograph on the left, though apparently the weather was not allowed to dampen spirits. The event, staged in a field near the *Blathwayt Arms*, Lansdown, was in aid of St Stephen's Church, says Ruth Boyling, of Weston. It is of special significance to her as her husband, Bill, then a child, features prominently, wearing a cap and sitting just above the lamp in the front row of the cart.

On the right, Pat Mills peers into the future and her revelations clearly come as something of a shock to her companions in this concert party group attached to Larkhall Congregational Church. This photograph from the 1950s was contributed by Gerald and Maureen Wall. Mrs Wall, then Maureen Jones, is on the left with Eric Leach and Frank Webber. On the right are Doreen Cocks and George Ives.

Sport

Once upon a time sport was played for fun or just for the exercise. Recent years have seen fundamental changes in the approach to sport, as commercial-isation, sponsorship and payment have moved in to dominate a growing segment of the sporting world. The new ethos is not necessarily bad for sport, but it is certainly making it different. The sporting subjects shown here illustrate a more innocent age.

When the Kennet and Avon Canal froze over at Bath in 1947 John Adams took to the ice on his skates and cut quite a dash. The occasion is treasured among the collection of Steve Adams.

Some of the 15,597 spectators roar on the City in one of Bath City's great FA Cup runs on 8th April 1943. They drew 2-2 with Aston Villa at Twerton Park in the quarter-finals (South), losing 3-4 on aggregate. Mavis Tait, MP for Frome, kicked off. She was later to commit suicide after visiting the horrific concentration camp at Belsen. The picture is from Leonard Partridge, of Eastfield Avenue, whose late brother, David, is seen here, one of the few fans to attend the wartime match bare-headed.

Those who wanted to swim to a high standard and take part in events with a competitive edge dived in at the deep end with Bath Dolphins Swimming Club. Mrs B. Cutting, of Keynsham, treasurer of the club, decided to collect an archive of old pictures of the club in action, and this is one sent in for the collection, recording the moment when a new member was taught to float.

In 1955 six swimmers using skin-diving equipment set out to cover the two miles of the Avon from Bathampton Weir to Pulteney Weir: only two made it. Recalling this event, Stanley Toogood, who was a process engraver at *The Bath Chronicle* for 45 years, says: "The event was organised by the Bath branch of the British Sub Aqua Club of which I was the secretary. Later I started the Reef Raiders Diving Group whose members river-searched for Bath police and also ran diver training courses for the youth and community services. The contestants in this first event were (standing) John Lacey and Cliff Hall, and (seated) Richard Whittingham, Don Parkes, myself and Albert Tusker. John Lacey won and I was the only other finisher.

Members of Bath Ladies' Rowing Club relax for a few minutes in this group photograph taken in about 1921 at their head-quarters at Forester Road, Bathwick. It was contributed by Janet Mohammed, formerly Janet Coward, who now lives in Cornwall. Her mother, Mrs K. E. Coward, who can be seen touching the centre of the crossed oars, became captain of the club.

Men's eights near the finishing line at Saltford Regatta in the final of the Jamaica Cup in 1960. Bristol Ariel narrowly beat Saltford-based Redcliffe Rowing Club. Keith Trivett, whose picture it is, says: "The first Bath Grand Regatta was raced between young gentlemen representing Bath, Bristol and Oxford over this course on a wet day in July 1849, with the public arriving at the riverbank either on foot, or by special

trains provided by the Great Western Railway or by the entrance opposite *The Globe* inn reserved for carriages. The event was renamed Saltford Regatta in 1890 and staged for many years by Avon, Bristol Ariel and a succession of Saltford-based clubs, interrupted only by two world wars. Building alterations at Saltford forced a transfer of the regatta to Bristol City Docks during the seventies with many of the original trophies now put up for competition at the Bristol Avon Regatta."

A Jack Russell on the pavement watches as attentively as the rest of them as Kingsmead House strongmen successfully pull their weight in a tug o' war contest against regulars at *The Green Tree* in Green Street in 1961. Pictured are Chris Daggar, Pat Symonds, Chris Symonds, Tommy Gifford, Micky Phillips, and Jerry Carp. Jacko was the pet dog of another of the Symonds family, Dave, and the photograph is from John Symonds.

Services

The concept of service runs deep and this group of photographs illustrates something of its range, from the simple to the giving up of life itself. It is quite often bound up with uniformed service which has the added pictorial advantage of illustrating changing fashions. Some of it is paid service, much voluntary. It reflects not only what society expects of its people, but what many people expect to do for society in times of peace and in the rarer times of war.

A sniper's bullet was waiting for Jack Sheppard, seen (right) mounted on the left of this detachment of the North Somerset Yeomanry taken in 1915. It was contributed by his son, Albert, who says: "Before the war broke out in 1914 my father broke and trained horses for the army and was often seen going through Weston with a string of horses tied head to tail. During the war, just before the regiment was due to depart for France, he was kicked by a horse and unable to leave with them. He departed later with a company of the Somerset Light Infantry, but was sadly wounded by a sniper and died in a Sheffield Hospital in 1917 when he was just 28."

Flamboyant moustaches and quite a few beards, not to mention several bemedalled chests of Boer War veterans, lend an air of distinction to this picture of Bath Post Office outdoor staff in 1908. It ranks high among the photographic treasures of Mary Randall, whose grandfather, Ernest Woolley, sits on the front row, fourth from the left. His first postal round was in Monkton Combe before moving on to Bathford for the next 20 years. When he left there for Combe Down in 1902, the people of Bathford presented him with a watch and chain, as well as a purse of sovereigns, at a special smoking concert at *The New Inn*.

Kitted out and ready for whatever hell the war would bring, from keeping watch on cold nights, building sandbag defences, spotting tell-tale leaks of light through blackout blinds, tackling incendiary bombs, to rescuing casualties from the ruins of their shattered homes, these Civil Defence air raid wardens parade in a cheerful group outside their headquarters at St Peter's Church, Twerton, in 1940 as the phoney war careered towards its abrupt transition to the real thing. Two small terriers even grace the picture, contributed by Pamela Gage of Frome, whose father was among those who formed this detachment.

Dispatch riders, on motorcycles or bicycles, formed an essential link in the command structure of Civil Defence, a structure badly affected on the first night of the 1942 blitz when the headquarters at Apsley House, Newbridge Hill, was put out of action by a bomb. Mrs I. James says this photograph of Combe Down Civil Defence Dispatch Riders was taken in 1941 with the leader, Les Knott, on the right of the picture. Bill Bale (ninth from the left) was killed at Royal Victoria Park in the blitz.

Bath City Police's new motorcycles and sidecars, numbers FB 9925 and 9926, were proudly put on display outside the old police station in Orange Grove in 1933 (right). Fred Hodges, of Cornwall, says the men on the left supplied the motorcycles, while also in the picture are the former chief constable, Captain Francis Peel, a descendant of Prime Minister Sir Robert Peel after whom 'Bobbies' were named, Alderman Aubrey Bateman, chairman of the Watch (police) Committee, and P. C. Bill Britten in a sidecar.

For those in peril on the sea: members of Bath Sea Cadet Corps attend a service, conducted by Commander Harrison, on board their whaler at Saltford Reach in 1943. George Randall, who went on to join the Merchant Navy two years later, is seen standing apart from the three at the stern of the boat, one of three which the cadets used to row or sail to Saltford on exercises.

To the beat of the drum, members of the 2nd Bath Company Boys' Brigade, attached to Oldfield Park Methodist Church, march across the Midland Bridge on a parade in 1944. Bernard Bond, of Whiteway, joined the Brigade as a bugler when he was 12, a year before this picture of his was taken.

This Albion was Bath's last open fire engine, photographed on its final day of service with Blue Watch at Bath Fire Station in the early sixties. Terry Jennings keeps the picture as one of the mementos of his years as a fireman before he retired from the service in 1974. He comments: "It saw service throughout the war, especially during the blitz of Bath. It was a thundering great thing. In those days they had more of a personality. There was a marvellous comradeship, just like a big family." He went on to become the city's senior driving examiner. Firemen with their trusty Albion are: (left to right, top row) Terry Jennings, Ivor Waldron, Roy Hulance, Ray Burgess and George Ham; (front, from left) Derek Kemp, Wally Weston, Mr Fitzpatrick, Dave Holly, Bill Mitchell, John Harding, Roger Davis and Dennis Farmer.

Industry and Workers

From cloth and corsets to cranes and cars, the trades and industries of Bath have been diverse, ranging in size from companies of international renown to one-man businesses. They have provided employment for Bath's own citizens as well as increasingly for people living in neighbouring towns and villages as the car has telescoped distances.

Bath has acted for centuries as a spa and tourist centre, with its associated shops, restaurants and hotels; more recently the Ministry of Defence took over as the city's major employer. Precision and heavy engineering, as well as furniture manufacture, have flourished. Many other industries, with their own special skills, have died as fashions have changed and technology has advanced; but major new concerns have moved in, often employing many people, such as the greatly enlarged hospitals, catering for patients from a wide area.

In this section we look at some of the shops and industries which have not survived, their role fulfilled or overtaken; at others which still exist and thrive; and at some of the entertainments and outings which people enjoyed in the course of their work.

Staff, proud of their safe, pasteurised milk, parade before their rounds in the early part of the century at the Bladud Buildings premises of the Bath and Somerset Dairy in this period piece photo from Edna Pine of Limpley Stoke. She says: "It was a working dairy, later taken over by Unigate, with 13 shops in and around Bath, some of which were bombed in the raids of 1942. My father was the assistant manager."

Before Bath Co-operative Society moved to its imposing store in Westgate Buildings, it had premises in Widcombe, as illustrated in this photograph from June Clarkson. The first branch opened at Twerton in 1888 and the movement extended into the heart of the city six years later. June's father, Edwin Purnell, stands on the right; he went on to manage the wine merchants, F.E. Norris in Brock Street. He was also a church organist in the city.

These two photographs, contributed by Mrs Lock, show workers at Bathford Paper Mills. On the left, a group of men put on their caps and the occasional bowler for a group photograph in about 1912, the year the firm was founded on the site where paper had already been produced for a century. The original building, owned by Bath Paper Mills, was destroyed by fire in the early 1900s. The firm was later sold to the firm of De La Rue, manufacturers of banknotes and security paper. In the photograph on the right, Mrs Lock's father, Ronald Gowan, is seen as a young worker with some of his colleagues. He is in the back row, second from the right, with his cap at a jaunty angle.

Ernest Williams opened one of the country's first self-service shops on the London Road in 1944, and later five launderettes as well as The Butterpat. He had left London in 1939 and went into business with Mr Batstone at the grocery shop in Saltford, illustrated here, before a spell of war service with the RAF. The Saltford shop was later turned into a private house.

He draws attention to the fact that the word 'Saltford' has been obliterated from the telephone number in the picture lest it should have given a clue on their whereabouts to any enemy parachutists.

Harold Moody of Southdown had a Saturday job as a boy, working for his uncle and aunt, George and Kitty Bennett, at their fruit, flower and vegetable shop in Chapel Row, a business which opened in the early years of the century. He recalls that on Saturdays and during school holidays he used to deliver goods from the shop to customers, carrying a large basket on each arm, until at the age of 11 he made a pair of trucks to make his task easier. Of the many pieces of china seen in the window, only one is still in the hands of the family.

Modern supermarkets may stock every imaginable kind of food from around the globe but there was something attractive about seeing a marble counter, well-stocked shelves, a chair to sit on and a friendly assistant waiting to serve you with whatever you wanted. This photograph, contributed by Clifford Storey, goes back to 1937 and shows the shop premises of

W. Adams & Son, grocers, provision merchants and wine stores, which was situated at No. 2, Argyle Street. The original shop had been at No. 4 since c.1875. In later years it was managed by Albert Smale until it closed in 1968.

A modern chemist's shop may not look all that different from this photograph from Ralph Oswick showing Tylee & Cooper's in Bridge Street. The shop, which opened in c.1870, was run by Edward Kingston from 1933 until it closed in 1972, It had a huge array of goods on display with posters advertising Polaroid sunglasses, Anadin, and both Wilkinson and Gilette razors. Hot water bottles dangle in a row from the ceiling, films are stacked high in the right-hand corner and there is a display of toothbrushes on the left. Among the products piled high on the counter are Gee's Linctus pastilles, Tyrozets and Colgate toothpaste – on special offer at two shillings and fourpence.

Stanley Waterson contributed this photograph (below) of his family's basket-manufacturing business at 24 Walcot Street. The picture shows the owner, George Waterson, on the right with an assistant. The photograph was apparently taken in 1900 just before Stanley was born. The firm later moved to the old soup kitchen in Chatham Row.

The poster for *The Daily Mirror* dates the picture on the right to 23rd or 25th March 1906. It shows Emily Brown and three of her children, Ivy, Stanley and Reuben, her youngest son, outside her newspaper and sweet shop in Twerton High Street just beneath the arch under Twerton Station. Jean Randall, Reuben's daughter, comments: "*The Bath Chronicle,* priced at ½d, was well advertised and so also was *The Bath Herald* [which merged with the *Chronicle* in 1926]. Reuben later represented Twerton on Bath City Council and is still well remembered and respected today."

A number of photographs dating back to the 1880s survive of this forge at Pent House Hill, Batheaston, where the Drewett family worked for more than two centuries. This 1906 picture of wheelwrights is in the archives of The Batheaston Society. The keen observer will note that the wooden sign board remains in place to this day, now somewhat faded.

The staff turned out to greet their giant new Davey Paxman boiler at Bath Steam Laundry in 1934, as recorded in this picture contributed by Hugh MacNiven. The firm was established in 1879 at St Peter's Terrace on the site of the old Twerton Tannery. The premises were later enlarged with a new frontage added in the 1950s. The business is now known as the Regency Laundry.

They were still ironing by hand in 1935 when this picture was taken in one of the work rooms at Bath Steam Laundry at Twerton, now The Regency Laundry. The room is still used for ironing, though now of course by machine. The firm has a large photographic archive and this picture, along with the one on the next page, was contributed by Hugh MacNiven.

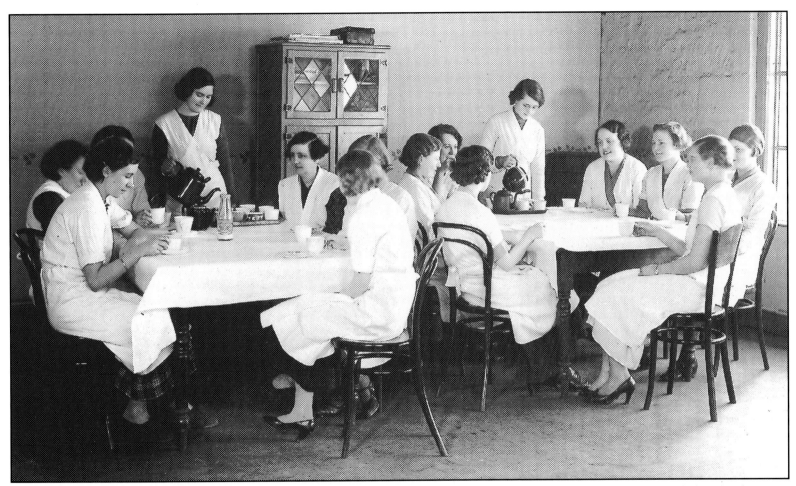

All looks rather sedate with not an ashtray in sight during this teabreak at Bath Steam Laundry's 'mess room'. Ironing is reputed to use up some 80 calories an hour so the break was probably well-earned. Note that the spotless overalls and tablecloths were of the same high standard as the laundry returned to customers.

Head gardener Edwin Perry (right) with his assistant gardeners armed with watering cans and sprays at The Trossachs, Bathampton, sometime before 1914. Edwin was the grandfather of Mrs P. Alford of Plymouth, who owns this picture. It recalls a period when staff were rather more plentiful than they were later to become and she says: "This picture must have been taken before 1914 as Edwin was with the Devonshire Regiment in France during the First World War and he died at Portsmouth from pneumonia on his way home in 1919, aged 41. He was buried in the churchyard of St Mary the Virgin at Marshfield."

The airy bindery at George Bayntun's Manvers Street premises 40 years ago. Describing the photograph, Nick Wellings says: "The bindery is still there and very active. Two of the apprentices at work at the back of the bindery are Raymond Tate and Alan Chivers, both of whom are now in charge of their own binderies at Period Bookbinders and Cottage Bindery and Print."

In the days when radios were called wirelesses these men were making cabinets for them at the Lower Bristol Road firm of W.T. Lock in 1928. Many of the wooden cabinets ranked as pieces of furniture in their own right and they also tended to be quite large, the signals coming from high aerials in gardens. The transistor and plastic were to change all that. This picture

came to Denise Chantry from her late uncle, Robert Field Cook, seen third from left in the workshop. With him, from left to right, were Bill Chivers, Bill Collins, Bert Hunt, Charlie Sizer and Stanley Milsom.

All is orderly, almost regimented, in the precision workshop of Horstmann Gear, photographed around 1930 when some 2,000 metal workers and engineers worked for various firms in the city. Norah Neal contributed this picture which shows her husband Frank, a member of Newbridge Male Voice Choir, in the third row on the right, next to the man standing up, Bert Andrews.

Head waiter Frank Burcombe stands behind the boar's head and other Christmas fare at the Empire Hotel before the Second World War. The building was taken over by the Admiralty in the war and has now been converted into flats. Frank's son Maurice recalls that the hotel staff ran into hundreds and that his father was often tipped £5, a worker's weekly wage in those days, to arrange for a porter to take a guest for treatment at the spa baths.

Cookery students concentrate as Eric Dixon passes on his skill as first chef instructor in the catering department of the former Bath Technical College. He was at the college for ten years before moving to the Admiralty. He and Miss M. Moseley later directed college catering students when they prepared a banquet at Longleat held in honour of the 80th birthday of the famous wine writer, André Simon, by the Bath and Bristol Wine and Food Society.

"Peace". 1918. 11 am. 11th day, 11th month. Harbutts' Plasticine Works Bathampton.

A precious memory of the coming of peace in 1918 is inscribed on this photograph taken at a Bathampton factory which had been converted to a war hospital. It is the Armistice Day memento at Harbutt's Plasticine and is in the collection of Meg Shine who appears as the little girl in the front row, second from right. Her brother, Jim Glass, is next to her on the right.

The world-famous Plasticine was developed by Bath art teacher William Harbutt in 1897 as a modelling medium for his students. Within three years it was being used on such a wide scale that commercial production began in an old flour mill at Bathampton. The business was sold and the Bathampton works closed in 1983.

Sir Isaac Pitman, pioneer of the shorthand system which was to facilitate so much for commerce worldwide, lived in Bath and set up his printing works in the city. It was, therefore, entirely appropriate that the Incorporated Shorthand Society should hold a conference in Bath; the members are pictured here in 1909 on a visit to the Roman Baths. Brian Coward says: "My grandmother, Mrs F.S. Coward, is standing in the lower right corner with the 'wedding cake' on her head."

This banner of the Bath branch of the Amalgamated Society of Railway Workers used to be marched through the city. It was last heard of when it was left in the loft of the *Royal Oak* on the Lower Bristol Road. Di Gibb's says her mother could remember it being carried in procession through Oldfield Park in 1913. Her grandfather, Joseph Hockey, a train driver, can be seen second from the right in the middle row.

Stothert and Pitt dominated heavy industry in Bath for decades, the Stothert family having set up the business in the late 18th century. With changes of partners the firm continued with extensive workshops until the 1980s when it was taken over by Robert Maxwell and subsequently died. It produced a wide range of goods, but was known world-wide for its cranes. Jack Nixey of Melksham is standing sixth from the left in his photograph of a works outing by charabanc.

At its height, the Admiralty, later the Ministry of Defence, directly employed almost 6,000 staff at Bath, but amid the tasks of designing ships and keeping the fleet at sea there was the occasional celebration, including this 1948 Christmas party. "I often think about those happy days," says Joy Fuller, who now lives in Sussex. The Admiralty moved to Bath on the outbreak of war in 1939 and took over hotels and schools before moving to its own establishments at Foxhill, Ensleigh and Warminster Road. Some staff have recently been transferred to the new complex at Abbey Wood, Bristol.

Smartly dressed shoppers bustle in Union Street and Cheap Street in this picture from Phyllis Arnold. Bunting is strung out, policemen patrol and a lone car seems almost to follow the tramlines. There is a suggestion of occasion about it, but just what has not been discovered. It is believed to have been taken between 1905 and 1907. Phyllis's father was manager of Hepworth's at the time and he is standing in the doorway on the left of the three figures. Her mother, aunt, sister and brother are in the first-floor front window. The Hepworth's site was later occupied by Boot's, Smith's and now Dixon's.

As a delivery boy crosses the road, unconcerned at any cars, Police Constable Rex Oatley directs the traffic at the bottom of the cobbled Milsom Street in the days when vehicles went up the street as well as down. He was to spend 30 years with Bath police, the borough force having been established in 1836 to take over the policing of the whole city, before retiring as

an inspector in 1955. Behind him is a branch of Huntley's grocery business, whose proprietor, Bill Huntley, became a barrister and was appointed to be the Recorder of Wells. This picture is framed at the home of Christine Oatley, daughter-in-law of the inspector.